G000164506

TRADITIONS AND CELEBRATIONS

HANUKKAH

by Jessica Server

raintree
a Capstone company — publishers for children

Raintree is an imprint of Capstone Global Library Limited, a company incorporated in England and Wales having its registered office at 264 Banbury Road, Oxford, OX2 7DY – Registered company number: 6695582

www.raintree.co.uk
myorders@raintree.co.uk

Edited by Erika L Shores
Designed by Dina Her
Original illustrations © Capstone Global Library Limited 2022
Picture research by Jo Miller
Production by Tori Abraham
Originated by Capstone Global Library Ltd
Printed and bound in India

978 1 3982 1298 5 (hardback)
978 1 3982 1362 3 (paperback)

British Library Cataloguing in Publication Data
A full catalogue record for this book is available from the British Library.

Acknowledgements
We would like to thank the following for permission to reproduce photographs:
AP Images: Corvallis Gazette-Times, Andy Cripe, 27; Getty Images: Comstock, 24, Jupiterimages, 5, kali9, 13, Sean Gallup/Staff, 29; Newscom: MAXPPP/WOSTOK PRESS, 19, Reuters/TIKSA NEGERI, 8, Yin Dongxun Xinhua News Agency, 20, ZUMA Press/Guido Montani, 23; Shutterstock: ChameleonsEye, 21, dossyl, 12, Golden Pixels LLC, 11, Ilker Murat Gurer, 9, Lisa F. Young, 14, Noam Armonn, 1, Pixel-Shot, 16, rSnapshotPhotos, 6, successo images, 17, tomertu, 10, Viktoria Hodos, Cover. Artistic elements: Shutterstock: Rafal Kulik.

Every effort has been made to contact copyright holders of material reproduced in this book. Any omissions will be rectified in subsequent printings if notice is given to the publisher.

CONTENTS

Words in **bold** are in the glossary.

WHAT IS HANUKKAH?

It is the first night of Hanukkah. The sun has set. A **Jewish** family lights a candle. They say a blessing. Then they share a meal.

Hanukkah is called the Festival of Lights. It celebrates a **miracle**. A very long time ago, Jews came to a **temple** in the city of Jerusalem. They needed oil to light the temple. They only found enough oil to last for one night. The oil burned for eight days and nights. This is why Hanukkah lasts for eight nights.

NDAY	TUESDAY	WEDNESDAY	THURSDAY
	1	2	3
7	8	9	10
		HANUKKAH BEGINS	
15	16	17	
22			HANUKKAH ENDS

WHEN IS HANUKKAH?

Jewish people use a special calendar. The calendar is a solar-lunar calendar. Solar means Sun. Lunar means Moon. This calendar uses the cycles of both the Sun and Moon.

Hanukkah starts on the 25th day of the ninth month of the Jewish calendar. The month is called Kislev. It is usually between late November and late December.

WHO CELEBRATES HANUKKAH?

Jewish people celebrate this holiday. They live all over the world. They follow the **religion** of **Judaism**. There are Jewish people in almost every country. Hanukkah celebrations are different from country to country.

Jewish people at a prayer service in the country of Ethiopia

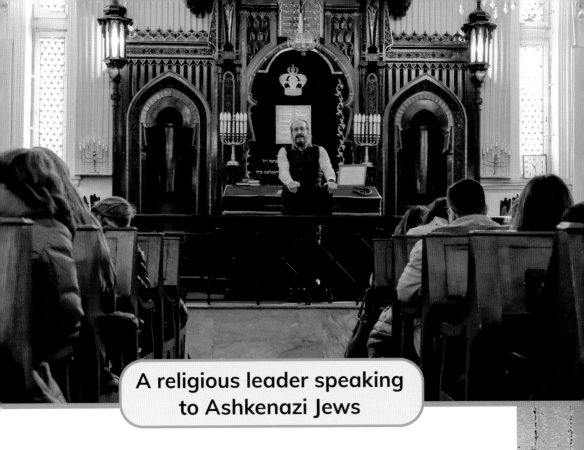

A religious leader speaking
to Ashkenazi Jews

Some Jewish **ancestors** came from
Europe. They are called Ashkenazi Jews.

Other Jewish ancestors came from the
Middle East and Spain. They are called
Sephardic Jews. They have different
traditions from Ashkenazi Jews.

HANUKKAH SYMBOLS

The menorah is the main symbol of Hanukkah. It is a candleholder with nine candles. The menorah is lit just before sunset on each night of Hanukkah.

A family lights the menorah on the last night of Hanukkah.

The shamash is the "helper" candle. It lights the other candles. On the first night, people use the shamash to light the first candle. One more candle is added to the menorah for each night of Hanukkah.

Blessings are said once the candles are in the menorah. Then the candles are lit. Some people say their blessings as they light the candles.

Children may get Hanukkah gelt as gifts. These chocolate coins are covered in gold and silver foil. Kids use them as game pieces when they play a game with a toy called a dreidel.

Dreidels are a kind of spinning top. They are wooden or plastic. There is one **Hebrew** letter on each of the four sides. Hebrew is the original language of Judaism.

A player spins the dreidel. The letter the dreidel lands on tells the player whether they win or lose gelt!

Latkes (right) are eaten with apple sauce and sour cream.

AT THE HANUKKAH TABLE

Jewish people eat fried foods at Hanukkah. Frying uses a lot of oil. The oil reminds Jewish people of the oil in the temple.

Many people eat latkes at Hanukkah. Latkes are potato pancakes. The potatoes are shredded and fried in hot oil. They are served with apple sauce and sour cream.

In Israel, people eat jam doughnuts called sufganiyot. They are topped with icing sugar. Jewish bakeries and delis around the world make them at Hanukkah.

In Colombia, Jewish people eat fried plantains at Hanukkah. Plantains are a fruit that looks like a banana.

People enjoy sufganiyot during Hanukkah.

gulab jamun

Jewish people in India fry doughnut balls called gulab jamun. They are served with syrup.

In Morocco, people eat fried dough called sfenj. These doughnuts are fluffy inside and are covered or dipped in honey or sugar.

HANUKKAH AROUND THE WORLD

Jewish people in different countries have their own ways of celebrating. For a long time, Jewish people in Ethiopia did not celebrate Hanukkah. Today many Ethiopian Jews light beeswax candles. They eat special North African dishes.

Jewish people in India visit **synagogues** during Hanukkah. People celebrate with their community at these places of **worship**. Indian Jews light wicks dipped in coconut oil or burn oil lamps. They eat Indian fried foods and special sweets.

A rabbi in India leads people in singing while lighting the menorah.

Many cities have big Hanukkah parties. There may be parades or festivals. Large menorahs light up public places. Crowds of people come to watch the menorahs being lit.

The city of Rome in Italy has a festival with a 6-metre (20-foot) menorah. Fried artichokes and special fried dough are common Hanukkah treats in Italy.

In Australia, November and December are summer months. People can celebrate Hanukkah outdoors. Jewish families spend time together in parks. They go to the beach. There may even be a Hanukkah street party!

HANUKKAH IN THE COMMUNITY

Different families in a community may celebrate Hanukkah in their own special ways. Some families go to synagogue.

A Jewish leader called a rabbi reads from the Torah. The Torah is the holy book of the Jewish religion. Each day of Hanukkah has its own reading.

A rabbi in a synagogue
in Rome, Italy

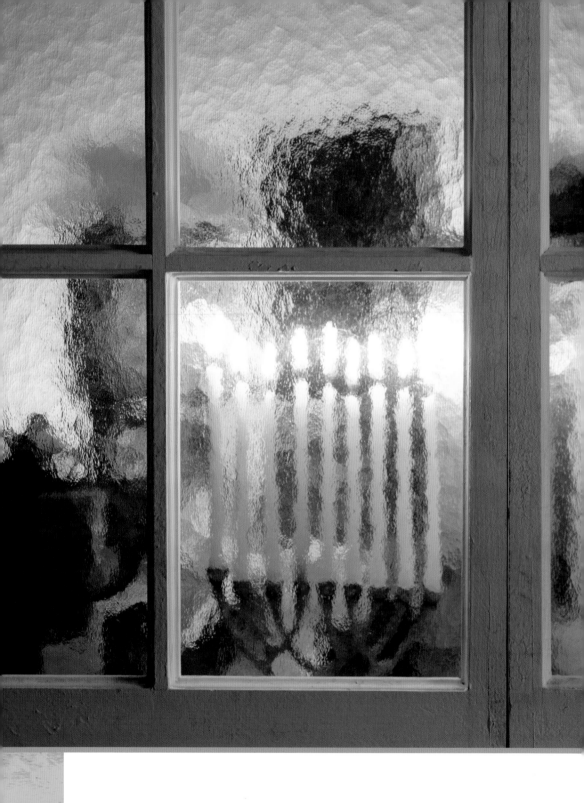

People put menorahs in their windows or near doorways. This lets other people see the candlelight from outside. It makes dark winter nights brighter. It also shows neighbours that a household is celebrating Hanukkah.

Some people give small Hanukkah gifts. One gift is given for each night of the holiday. Not all families choose to give gifts.

Jewish people may sing songs together during Hanukkah. One Hanukkah song is called "Maoz Tzur". It is sung after the candles are lit.

Singing "Hanukkah, Oh Hanukkah" reminds Jewish people of the joy of lighting the menorah and having a fun party. Another song that children sing is called "I Have a Little Dreidel".

Jews in Turkey sing "Ocho Kandelikas". This means eight little candles. The song is part of the Sephardic tradition.

HANUKKAH AT HOME

It is now the eighth night of Hanukkah. All the candles on the menorah are lit. The room glows. People say the last night's blessing. They sing together. Children play the dreidel game one last time.

The holiday is now over. Jewish people everywhere celebrated the miracle of Hanukkah. They followed their own special traditions. The Festival of Lights brought joy to Jewish people around the world.

GLOSSARY

ancestor family member who lived a long time ago

culture people's way of life, ideas, art, customs and traditions

Hebrew language of Judaism

Jewish people who follow the religion or culture of Judaism

Judaism religion based on a belief in one God and the teachings of a holy book called the Torah

miracle event that cannot be explained

religion set of spiritual beliefs that people follow

synagogue building where Jewish people come together to pray

temple building used for worship

tradition custom, idea or belief passed down through time

worship show love or honour to a higher being

FIND OUT MORE

BOOKS

Celebrating Jewish Festivals (Celebration Days), Liz Miles (Raintree, 2016)

Celebrations Around the World: The Fabulous Celebrations You Won't Want to Miss, Katy Halford (DK Children, 2019)

Children Just Like Me: A New Celebration of Children Around the World, DK (DK Children, 2016)

WEBSITES

www.bbc.co.uk/bitesize/topics/z478gwx/articles/zb33pg8
Learn more about different celebrations.

www.dkfindout.com/uk/more-find-out/festivals-and-holidays
Find out more about festivals and holidays around the world.

INDEX